Please return/renew this item by the last
date shown. Books may also be renewed
by phone or Internet.

 www.rbwm.gov.uk/web/libraries.htm

☎ 01628 796969 (library hours)

☎ 0303 123 0035 (24 hours)

Published by Evans Brothers Limited
2A Portman Mansions
Chiltern Street
London W1U 6NR

© Evans Brothers Limited 2002
Reprinted 2003, 2005

Produced for Evans Brothers Limited by
White-Thomson Publishing Ltd,
Bridgewater Business Centre,
210 High Street, Lewes, East Sussex BN7 2NH

Printed in China by WKT Company Limited.

Editor: Anna Lee
Consultant: Norah Granger
Designer: Tessa Barwick
Map Illustration: The Map Studio

Cover (centre): Florence Nightingale at Scutari Hospital.
Cover (top left): a wounded soldier and friend on the
  battlefront during the Crimean War.
Cover (top right): Florence Nightingale attends to a patient
  in Scutari Hospital.

The right of Stewart Ross to be identified as the author of
this work has been asserted by him in accordance with the
Copyright, Designs and Patents Act 1988.

British Library Cataloguing in Publication Data

Florence Nightingale. - (Start-up history)
  1.Nightingale, Florence, 1820-1910
  2.Nurses - England - Biography - Juvenile literature
  3.Crimean War - Medical care - Great Britain -
  Juvenile literature
  I.Title
  610.7'3'092

ISBN: 0237 52410 4

Acknowledgements: The publishers would like to thank
the Florence Nightingale Museum, London, for their
assistance with this book.

Picture Acknowledgements: Bridgeman Art Library
9 *(right)*; Bridgeman Art Library/British Museum 8;
Bridgeman Art Library/Private Collection *(cover, centre)*,
10 *(top)*, 12 *(bottom)*, 15; Corbis 17, 19 *(right)*; Florence
Nightingale Museum 11, 18; Fotomas Index 19 *(left)*;
Mary Evans Picture Library *(cover, top right and top left)*
4, 5, 9 *(top)*, 10 *(bottom)*, 12 *(top)*, 13, 14; P&O Art
Collection 7; Topham Picturepoint 16.

Contents

Florence Nightingale, a famous nurse

▶ This is Florence Nightingale.
She was born long ago, in the year 1820.

How are her clothes different from modern clothes?

long ago   year   modern

▲ **Florence** was a famous nurse.
She worked in hospitals like this one.

famous   nurse   hospitals   5

Florence goes to help

In 1854, Great Britain went to war with Russia. The war was far away, in the Crimea.

Florence went to nurse the injured soldiers.

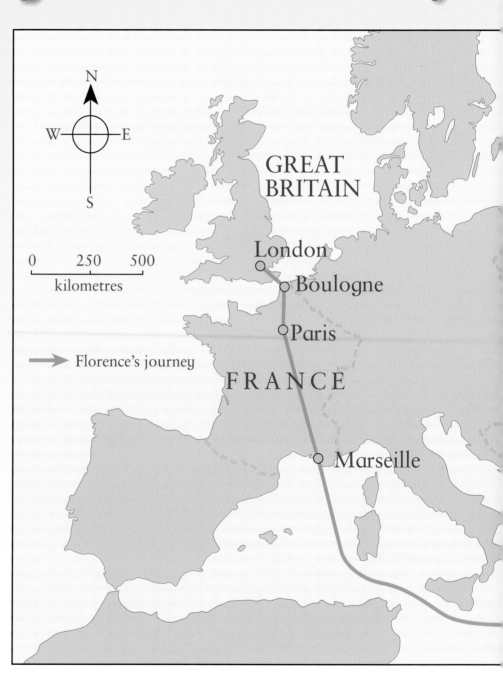

Florence's journey

Great Britain war Russia Crimea

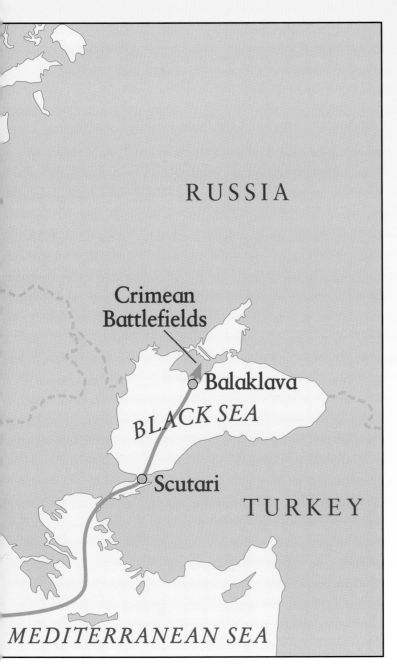

RUSSIA

Crimean
Battlefields

Balaklava

BLACK SEA

Scutari

TURKEY

MEDITERRANEAN SEA

◀ **This map shows her journey.
She travelled by land and sea.**

▼ **Florence sailed in this ship.**

injured   soldiers   map   sailed   **7**

Why did Florence go to the war?

▼ This is a painting of a battle in the Crimean War. What weapons are the soldiers using?

painting   battle

▲ This soldier is helping his friend who has been hurt.

Nurses were needed at the war.

► This man, Sidney Herbert, asked Florence to go and help. She said "yes" straight away.

weapons   hurt

Florence and the horrible hospital

▶ **This is the hospital where Florence worked. It was in a place called Scutari.**

Scutari was a long way from the Crimea.

◀ **Injured soldiers went to Scutari by boat.**

Scutari   boat

▼ **This is the inside of a hospital during the war.**

Scutari hospital looked like this, too.
It was crowded, dirty and smelly.
How many injured soldiers can you see?

crowded   dirty   smelly

Florence goes to work

▶ **Florence needed** medicines **from Britain. They were sent by ship.**

◀ **Queen Victoria helped Florence. She sent kind words and presents for the soldiers.**

medicines

▼ **Here is Florence talking to a soldier in Scutari Hospital.**

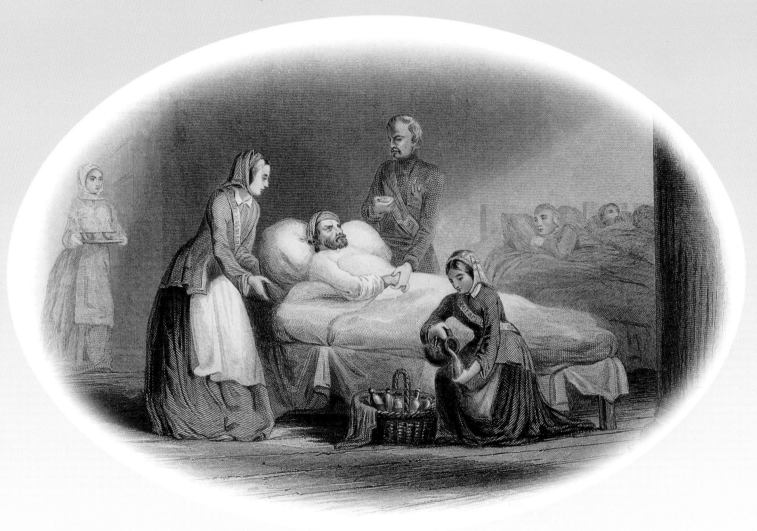

She worked to make it cleaner and healthier. How is the hospital in this picture different from the picture of the hospital on page 11?

cleaner   healthier

How did Florence help?

▲ This is the inside of Scutari hospital after Florence had cleaned it up.

There are clean sheets on the beds and a stove to keep the patients warm.

patients

Florence **trained** other nurses at Scutari.

▼ This nurse is working near a battle.

How can you tell that this **photograph**
was taken long ago?

trained   **photograph**

Nursing changes

After she returned from the war, Florence started
a school for nurses.

Here is Florence with some of the nurses from her school.
The nurses are wearing their uniforms.

after   school   uniforms

This is a nurse at work today.
She is wearing a plastic apron.

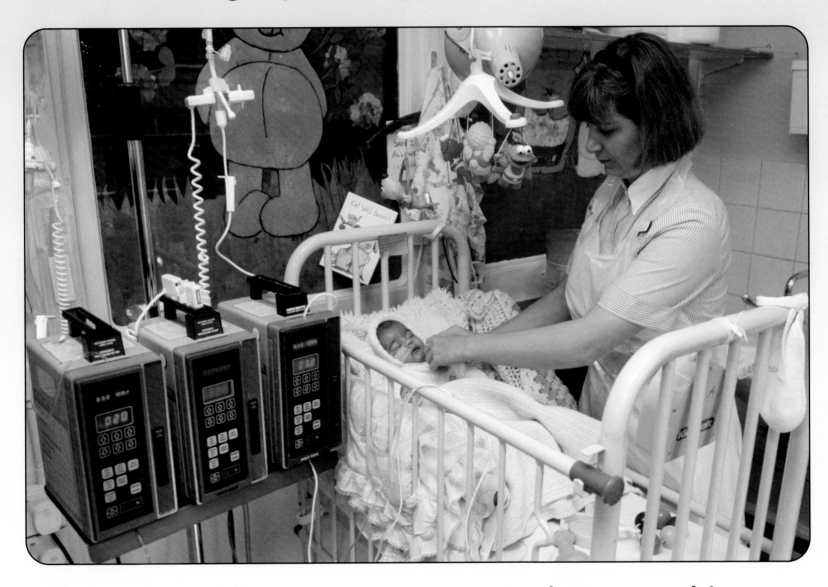

What other differences can you see between this
picture and the pictures of the hospitals from the past?

today   plastic   differences   past   17

How do we know about Florence Nightingale?

General Hospital
Balaklava
June 7/56

My Lord
Once more I venture to trouble you with the request that you will favor me with your instructions viz. how you would wish the remainder of those stores, intrusted to my charge by the Crimean Fund Committee, to be disposed of, as we are now clearing out all stores.
I have the honor to be
My Lord
Your Lordship's obliged & obedt servt
Florence Nightingale
I shall not be able to effect the separation of the Crimean Fund Stores
0865

Florence Nightingale died almost 100 years ago.

We can find out about Florence by reading the letters she wrote.

◀ This is a letter Florence wrote to Sidney Herbert from Balaklava.
You can find Balaklava on the map on pages 6 and 7.

died   letters

SAVED BY A FAMOUS NURSE.

A VETERAN'S REMINISCENCE.

[BY TELEGRAPH.—OWN CORRESPONDENT.]

Christchurch, Thursday.

When a youth of 17 years of age Edward Bond, now a resident of Christchurch, was engaged as interpreter to the police at Kadakoi, near Balaclava. Under the rigors of the climate he broke down, and after a brief illness was given up as dead by the army doctors in the rude hospital. He was covered over with an army blanket, and over his head the army card announced that he was to be transferred to the "dead tent." On that day Miss Florence Nightingale arrived at Balaclava, and made her first inspection of the hospital. Bond's bed was the first inside the door, and Miss Nightingale paused before it, read the card, and then said softly. "What a pity to die so young." She went to the head of the bed to turn down the blanket, and at once said, "Why, he is not dead." Efforts were made to secure his recovery, and ultimately Bond walked out of the hospital and resumed his duties.

"All that I learnt," said the veteran to a reporter, "from the man in the bed next to mine. If Miss Nightingale had not seen me I would have been taken out to the dead tent. I saw Miss Nightingale just before she was taken ill herself, and I thanked her. She remembered me, saying, 'Oh, you are the boy they ordered to be buried.'"

▲ **Newspapers** and **magazines** from long ago tell us about Florence.

▼ **We can learn about Florence from old paintings and photographs, too.**

newspapers　　**magazines**　　**19**

The story of

Use these pictures and words to tell the story of Florence Nightingale.

nurse sailed Crimea soldier war

Florence Nightingale

Where did she go?

What did she do there?

Why do we remember her today?

hospital   cleaner   Scutari   school

New history words and words about Florence Nightingale listed in the text:

after	dirty	long ago	past	smelly
battle	famous	magazines	patients	soldiers
boat	Great Britain	map	photograph	today
cleaner	healthier	medicines	plastic	trained
Crimea	hospital	modern	Russia	uniforms
crowded	hurt	newspapers	sailed	war
died	injured	nurse	school	weapons
differences	letters	painting	Scutari	year

Background Information

FLORENCE NIGHTINGALE

Florence Nightingale (1820-1910) is remembered for her work as a nurse during the Crimean War. Highly-strung and determined, at an early age Florence set her mind on becoming a nurse. The profession was then almost exclusively the reserve of women of low status. Finally winning parental approval for her career, Florence trained in Germany and worked in London before volunteering to lead a band of 38 nurses to the Crimea in 1854. A formidable organiser (but a poor nurse), Florence set about bringing order to the army hospital at Scutari. However, the appalling death rate there did not subside until a commission had identified and eliminated diseases stemming from the hospital's lamentable sanitation. Florence fell seriously ill in the Crimea and after her return home, now a national hero, she took to her bed for nine years. She devoted the rest of her life to the nursing profession, especially training and army nursing.

THE CRIMEAN WAR

Fought against Russia in alliance with France, the Crimean War (1854-6) soon became a byword for incompetent management and leadership. Anglo-French forces were sent to the Crimea to take the Russian port of Sebastopol and prevent further Russian expansion into the crumbling Ottoman Turkish Empire. A second, Baltic front was opened up to deter Russian expansion into Scandinavia. Ultimately, both campaigns achieved their objectives, although at considerable cost in terms of lives lost and political and military careers ruined. 4,600 British soldiers were killed in battle and 17,500 died of disease. Mounting criticism of the way the war was conducted forced the resignation of Lord Aberdeen's government in 1855.

BALAKLAVA

Balaklava, a small port in the south of the Crimea, was the scene of a major battle of the Crimean War in 1854.

Parents and Teachers

The balaclava helmet, a woollen hood that covers the ears and neck, was worn by soldiers during the Crimean War. It is still used today.

SIDNEY HERBERT

Lord Sidney Herbert (1810-61) served as a reforming minister in the war office from 1845 onwards. He established Aldershot as the major army base in Britain and was responsible for the radical step of sending Florence Nightingale (a personal friend) and her nurses to help at Scutari.

Possible Activities:

Draw pictures of Florence, Scutari and the Crimea.
Make a wall map of Florence's journey to the Crimea.
Make a class frieze timeline.
Find a modern nurse willing to talk to the class about her work. What does she think of Florence Nightingale?
List objects, buildings etc. from the time of Florence Nightingale.

Compare newspaper articles from today and from the nineteenth century. How are they different?

Some Topics for Discussion:

Which tells us more about Florence Nightingale, letters or paintings? What are the advantages and disadvantages of each?
Can we trust 'eyewitnesses'?
What else could Florence have done with her life?
Did she deserve to be a celebrity?
What made her a celebrity?
Discuss other famous people from the past.

Further Information

BOOKS

FOR CHILDREN

Please Help, Miss Nightingale! by Stewart Ross (Evans, 1997)
Don't Say No to Flo! by Stewart Ross (Hodder Wayland, 2002)
Florence Nightingale by Jane Shuter (Heinemann, 2001)
Florence Nightingale by Peggy Burns (Hodder Wayland, 1999)
Get a Life! Florence Nightingale by Philip Ardagh (Macmillan, 1999)

FOR ADULTS

Florence Nightingale by Cecil Woodham-Smith (Constable, 1950)
Florence Nightingale, Avenging Angel by Hugh Small (Constable, 1998)
Florence Nightingale: Letters from the Crimea by Sue Goldie (Mandolin, 1996)

WEBSITES

http://www.florence-nightingale.co.uk
http://www.dnai.com/~borneo/nightingale
(American and idiosyncratic, yet touching.)
http://www.spartacus.schoolnet.co.uk/REnightingale.htm

PLACES TO VISIT

Florence Nightingale Museum, London
Bethlem Royal Hospital & Archives, Beckenham, Kent
British Red Cross Museum, London
National Army Museum, London

Index